iChange

iChange
Nathan Garber

Making Change Work for You!

Copyright © 2011 Nathan Garber. All rights reserved.

iChange
Making Change Work for You!

Editor: Philip R. Byler

Printed in the USA

ISBN: 978-0-9847653-6-2

All Rights Reserved. This book is protected by the copyright laws of the United States of America. This book may not be copied or reprinted for commercial gain or profit. The use of short quotations is permitted. Permission will be granted upon request. The author guarantees all contents are original and do not infringe upon the legal rights of any other person or work.

Prepared for Publication By

PUBLICATIONS

Palm Tree Publications is a Division of Palm Tree Productions
www.palmtreeproductions.com
PO BOX 122 | KELLER, TX | 76244

To contact the Author:
nathan@cornerstoneplatinum.com
(406) 407-8604

Acknowledgements

As with any worthwhile or successful project there is always more than one person involved. This book is no different. I've been encouraged to do this book by more people than I can name ... so thanks to all of you! There are several people very directly involved that I want to thank by name.

To Wendy, I pray for you to be as successful as you are constantly making others. You are excellent in every way. You did an amazing job on the cover and formatting the pages. I am delighted with what you have done.

To Mr. Byler, I am glad to have someone that can make my writing readable! You patiently listened and kept making changes to help it say what I wanted it to say. Thank you!

Most of all, I am grateful to my wife, Kathy! Thank you for unleashing all your skills in making sure I can put to paper my thoughts and feelings. I appreciate the hours you spent reading and rereading the manuscript giving me feedback that well, I couldn't pay you what it was worth! I'm not sure what it would be like having someone sit in front of me going, "Tell me what I mean. You know what I'm thinking right?" But you helped in every meaningful way possible. I love you and I love working with you!

iChange

When you learn to embrace the power of change, you are on the road to making change work for you!

Contents

7	**Introduction**
13	Chapter One **A Time for Change**
23	Chapter Two **Change is an Opportunity**
35	Chapter Three **Hanging by a Thread**
51	Chapter Four **Enduring Change**
59	Chapter Five **Evaluating Yourself**
67	Chapter Six **Engaging Your State**
81	Chapter Seven **Breaking the Cycle**
97	Chapter Eight **Releasing Yourself**
107	Chapter Nine **Created For a Purpose**
113	**Epilogue**
123	**Bonus Material**

iChange

Introduction

The interesting thing about life is it never stays the same! Everything is always in a state of flux. Things are always changing. Throughout the pages of this book, I share insights on how to make change work for you. Because I have experienced so much change, I drew many examples from my own life experience.

My goal in writing this book is to help you be able to change effectively. I want to help you minimize the frustration that comes when things don't work out the way you thought they would or should. I want you to embrace the principles of dynamic, disruptive change and experience how this can bring success in your own life.

There is a way to live in the middle of shifting circumstances and constant change without feeling as though your life is out of control. There is a way you can face each day with confidence. For this to happen, you need to be willing to make change work in your favor. Understanding this will make a tremendous difference in your life.

Throughout the book I candidly offer experiences from my life, first as an Amish boy, then later as a young man in the Mennonite culture. These are very conservative communities, both socially and religiously. They are restrictive and tightly controlled environments. These constraints are not always easy for a young man to accept; especially when his dreams and desires reach beyond their boundaries.

Within this book I use examples of several unpleasant situations which have occurred throughout my journey. These do not give a complete picture of Amish and Mennonite life. I am who I am because of what I

Introduction

was taught as a boy. So, from the outset, let me assure you, I greatly value what I gained within their culture.

In spite of any shortcomings I may communicate, I sincerely appreciate my heritage and the ideals I learned in my youth. Both the Amish and the Mennonites hold to community in a way that is hard for people outside of those circles to imagine. They genuinely care for each other and look after each other's interests in profound ways.

At twelve years of age, I fell thirty feet down a silo chute, landing on the concrete floor below. The impact left me unconscious, with my upper back and right shoulder broken. Costs from the ten day stay in the hospital were staggering, and since the Amish do not participate in insurance programs, paying the bill was a huge burden for my family.

Word went out that we needed help, and people from across our community pitched in to help us pay our bill. More than just our local community responded. People from Amish communities in other states also contributed. The Amish and Mennonite people don't just talk about helping each other, they actually do it. This is a remarkable value I hope to instill in my own family and practice throughout my life.

In the fall they work together harvesting crops. I remember in my early teens getting up early, doing morning chores, and then going to a neighboring farm to help bring in their crops all day. We not only worked together; we enjoyed working together. In all honesty, it was fun. The camaraderie, the fellowship, the sense of accomplishment we shared made these days both enjoyable and profitable.

At the time, I didn't realize I was also learning to value hard work, a team spirit, and an awareness of other people's needs. These foundations have helped me become the man I am today.

I was taught honesty and integrity as a standard of life. Sunday after Sunday, I heard the stories of the Bible in church. As a young child, I often thought it was boring. Today, as a person of faith, I realize how much this helped me through hard times I encountered later in my life.

Introduction

Being part of that culture, I may have missed out on certain opportunities, but in other areas of my life, I realize I have great advantages. The lessons I learned deep down continue to serve me well as a businessman and an entrepreneur.

Today, I am profoundly grateful for my parents, Amos and Katie Garber, both of whom worked diligently to give me the very best life they could provide. They instilled in me the values that made them who they are, not as Amish, but as people.

My dad passed away in 2004. My mom continues to inspire me to be true to the never changing values by which she has lived her life and has instilled in mine. I've watched her go through some very difficult times; times that would cause other people to become utterly discouraged. She never allowed discouragement to win.

My mother has always focused on what was good rather than what was going wrong. This has always inspired me to look for the silver lining and seek opportunities even when facing obstacles.

iChange

My mother is an amazing woman who is unmoved by what other people think. She has lived her life with integrity and a dignity that brings honor to her family, to the memory of her husband, to her community, and especially to me. She is a shining example of goodness and faith, one which anyone would do well to follow.

Chapter One

Time for Change

I distinctly remember a change I chose which reprogrammed my whole life. It began with a meeting in my pastor's garage. My wife, Kathy and I were part of a conservative Mennonite community, and as such, valued the counsel and wisdom of our leadership. On that particular day, the pastor met with me to discuss several questions I had regarding a project I was planning to do.

I was totally unprepared for the change that meeting initiated. However, life sometimes brings you into unexpected circumstances which require you to make hard choices. This was one of those moments.

iChange

I had been given the opportunity to bid on a very large project; one which would produce significant income and vastly improve the quality of our lives. My pastor was not impressed with the opportunity, however. Rather, he was critical and even somewhat hostile toward my enthusiasm and ambition. In our Mennonite community, ambition was not viewed as being completely without merit. Too much ambition, however, or ambition that stretched traditional boundaries was a violation of our cultural restraints.

In a previous conversation he had cautioned me about my ambition, but on this occasion he said he heard from God that I was not to pursue this opportunity. I was once again told to submit to something I could not understand—a directive that made no sense. I was stunned by his response. I left his presence disappointed and frustrated.

I was overwhelmed by the emotions rushing through me. My head was spinning; my mind racing ahead toward an uncertain future. The conversation left no doubt in my mind, we were finished as Mennonites.

A Time for Change

The most natural progression for people who depart from Amish life is to connect with the Mennonites. This we had done some time before. Now we were choosing to leave Mennonite life as well. We felt our lives could no longer continue to advance, bound by the religious restrictions which accompanied this lifestyle.

The difference between their perspective and the values we held was too great. I wanted to be able to teach my children principles for successful living and I just could not bring myself to tell them to accept things which have no lasting value.

It was important to me for my life to count in a much larger sense than I was experiencing. The gap between my desires and the strict standards of the church was just too wide.

Knowing I wanted to live life to the fullest, breaking with the Mennonite church was the only answer for me. Still, I was gripped with fear. I had no idea what would happen next, where we would go, or what we would do. The Amish and Mennonite lifestyles were all we had ever known or experienced.

iChange

Kathy and I both grew up in the Amish community, immersed in the ultra-conservative lifestyle of the plain people—she in one place, I in another. When our paths crossed and our changing lives came together, neither of us had any idea where our journey would take us. It had taken us into the conservative Mennonite community where our family, our friends and our faith all blended together. Now this was about to change—a radical, disruptive, life-altering change.

The Amish and Mennonite peoples come from a common heritage. Few people realize that the Amish faith was actually a step away from the Mennonites several centuries ago. Because the Amish appear to be much more traditional, clinging to old-fashioned practices such as horse and buggies and shunning the use of electricity, the assumption is that they came first and the Mennonites came out of them.

This is untrue. In fact, the Amish broke away from the Mennonites and there are some segments of the Mennonite community that are far more conservative than others.

A Time for Change

While there are real differences, people from outside of these cultures seldom recognize or understand them. In some instances, the Mennonites are barely distinguishable from the Amish by outsiders, because their lifestyle, dress, and demeanor are so similar.

So, in stepping away from the Amish, we had not stepped very far, at least not initially. Little by little, we moved from more conservative to less conservative circles embracing change as we went. We were always reaching for where life would take us, yet never truly disengaging from what we had always known.

With time, Kathy and I grew personally in so many ways—ways which were different from many of the people around us. We were reaching for a change from the lifestyle we were living and we wanted to continue to do so. We became acutely aware we did not really fit in where we were. Our lives had shifted. They had taken on a new perspective. However, until that meeting with my pastor, I had not realized how much we had changed. From that point forward, however, I was certain. It was time for change. We would be moving into an entirely different place.

iChange

The late afternoon drive back to our home seemed exceptionally long. As I drove, I contemplated telling my wife we could no longer be a part of the Mennonite church. I knew asking her to leave the Mennonite church would turn our lives completely upside down. Her response was more shock than fear.

When we made the decision, the sense of loss was immediate for both of us. We loved these people so much, and we had built some very close relationships among them. There were so many uncertainties about what leaving this community would mean for our lives. We embraced the change, not knowing the impact or fully comprehending the outcome.

As far back as we could remember, we had been told that if we left the Amish and Mennonite communities, it would be over for us. Becoming part of another church would make no difference; the place we were going would be evil. Prior to this, each time we had made a significant move, it had been within these communities.

This time was different, however. We were leaving everything that had been remotely familiar or comfortable to us. There would be no support

A Time for Change

community, no circle of sympathetic friends who would agree with us or encourage us in our choice.

We had to make this decision on our own. The choice was ours and ours alone. If we backed away at this point, we knew we would not go any further. It was a crossroads that required a conscious decision.

Change can be difficult to embrace, yet change is with us all the time. It comes in different shapes and sizes, and while the circumstances which produce change are different, everyone goes through them.

There are only two basic types of change people must respond to. One comes when things happen that are out of your control. The other is set in motion by change you choose. Whether or not you are aware of changes taking place, you will experience both types over the course of your lifetime. In fact, you will experience a lot of changes.

At any given point in time, when you take a step back to look at your life, you can see the results of changes you've made. Sometimes you like what you see. Other times you don't. But the changes you make today affect your future in significant ways, even though you may not understand how or why at the time you decide to make a change.

> **Every circumstance is filled with opportunity.**

Every circumstance is filled with opportunity, whether it is one we develop or one that just happens. Recognizing that opportunity lies hidden within every circumstance can be difficult, especially when the circumstance is out of your control. Still, changing circumstances call for choices to be made, and the choices you make always determine the future you will experience. Even when you do not consciously choose a direction, a choice is made. Then, the direction chooses you.

Leaving our close-knit faith group was a difficult choice, but it had to be made. We either had to surrender our values and remain tied to something we no longer believed in, or follow the path that was really in our hearts.

A Time for Change

The hard part was finding the strength to face the consequences of our choice. We knew there would be criticism and condemnation. We tried to prepare ourselves for the certain rejection from our friends and family, aware that they really did not understand what we were choosing to do.

The alternative would have been to do what was easy, remain in the Mennonite community and try to get along—trying to please other people. But life had already taken us so much farther than the constraints we were born into. We had made choices along the way that allowed us to experience so many different things.

Settling for something less now was not really an option. We had already made many hard choices, each allowing us a progression toward a better life. I really did not want to stop at this point.

With my wife at my side, we agreed to move forward. The unknowns we would face, we would face together.

iChange

Chapter Two

Change is an Opportunity

Passion is what drives me. Passion generates pursuit. I want my life to count for something more than a comfortable niche in a marginalized community. If we had continued within the Amish lifestyle, this story would never have been written. Our journey would not be an encouragement to anyone.

I will never forget what it was like growing up. Amish culture is a lifestyle carved out of the past. It is a bit of a time-warp, drawn from an earlier civilization but planted in a twentieth-century world. We farmed with equipment that had long since been surpassed by agricultural technology. We plowed, planted, and harvested our crops with horse-drawn machines. For

iChange

transportation we relied on buggies and wagons, never opting to own automobiles or other modern means of travel. As much as was possible, we were removed from the mainstream of the surrounding cultures. We had contact with them, talked with them, traded with them, and tolerated them. However, we did not mingle with them unnecessarily. To me, I felt as though I was living in a box. At times I felt like I would explode if things didn't change.

As a young Amish boy growing up on a farm, I would sometimes lay in the grass in our front yard, it was warm and smelled sweet. I would watch the jet planes flying overhead, thirty or thirty-five thousand feet in the air, and dream of flying. I would daydream for hours, imagining what it would be like to be up there flying free. But flying is not an option for an Amish boy. Buggies don't fly.

Flying wasn't my only dream. I also developed a genuine desire to help people in significant ways. I wanted to really make a difference in other people's lives. But as an Amish boy there was no context for that either. Making a difference in other people's lives was

Change is an Opportunity

limited to a very narrow framework. We were raised to love our neighbor and we helped each other with work or in times of crisis. But impacting someone's life was certainly not possible on the grand scale of my dreams.

For instance, if someone needed help on their farm I could go and help them complete their work. Or, if one of their family members became sick, I could help them in some way or another, picking up the responsibility for some chores or other work that needed to be done. But in the context of influence, in the context of having the resources or knowledge to help people on a large scale, I had no grid—no way of stretching that far.

So I constantly found myself wondering what my life was going to be like. A growing dissatisfaction found its way into my soul. I wanted more. I knew I was born for more than life on an Amish farm and I wanted to reach for it. I just didn't know how.

As I was growing up, I watched my dad's life. I listened to stories he told about when he was young. During my teens and into my early twenties, it seemed he was frustrated with much of his life. Back then I didn't pick up on the true cause of his frustration. I thought he was just being irritable, or maybe he was having a bad day.

The older I grew, the more I realized his frustration came from consequences of the choices he had made. He chose to stay in the Amish community, chose to accept those restraints and honor the culture he was raised in, but he was a dreamer too. He just didn't allow himself to pursue them.

Amish culture places a lot of limitations on a man; limitations which I now realize my dad did not particularly appreciate. At one point in time, when he was younger, he had tried to break away from the constraints of the only life he knew. But for reasons known only to him, he came back and stayed until he died. As I watched him, I resolved not spend the rest of my life looking at the back end of a horse.

So many times during those years, I too felt the restrictions that accompanied our lifestyle. There was not enough room or space for me to become who I was meant to be. I feared I might never be able to do what I honestly wanted to do. Even when I left the Amish and

Change is an Opportunity

joined the Mennonites, I did not feel the freedom I was longing for. It seemed a safe choice. Better, but only a little better.

Then I met Kathy, and life took a fresh turn. Kathy and I were married in the Mennonite tradition. We were so much in love and looked forward to having a family with great expectation. But the thought of having a child just amplified my sense of uncertainty.

Soon we were expecting our first child, and I realized even more how much I wanted our children to have a different life than I had known. My wife shared my concerns. We wanted our children to have better opportunities, broader choices, and greater potential than those we could give them among our own people.

Having a second child only heightened our restlessness. Now we had two children and we knew they would grow up quickly. More than ever, I wanted them to be able to reach their maximum potential in life. But deep down I knew this was not possible, not as long as we were obliged to live under the rules and regulations of our tight-knit community.

iChange

We knew we couldn't stay where we were. We had to break free from the tension that existed between our past and our future. Radical change was the only answer. We just did not know how or when it would come.

Life is filled with opportunities. Sometimes we dream and feel we know just where we want to be and what we want our lives to look like. Unfortunately, we have little or no understanding of the process we must go through to get there. We don't know what life will throw at us on the journey, making it hard when unexpected things occur. It's just not possible to have a plan for every situation you will face along the way.

Hidden inside insurmountable obstacles are opportunities for change.

Your dreams and plans are clear. Everything seems to be going well. Then, life throws you a "curve," a challenge you never imagined, a problem far bigger than your plan. These are the things

Change is an Opportunity

that force you to grow. They look like insurmountable obstacles, but hidden inside are opportunities for change. Unpredictable, yes! Difficult, absolutely! But still, they are opportunities if you will let them be. Such challenges shape your character, develop your potential, and intensify your determination.

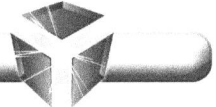

Talk about curve balls ... at four years of age, our oldest son Tristan was diagnosed with end-stage kidney failure. He was born with posterior urethral valves. It is something a simple surgery can fix. But his kidneys and bladder had been severely damaged before the doctors discovered these tiny valves. They were the cause of his kidney infections, frequent high fevers, and being miserably sick in the first two years of his life. It was a heart-wrenching experience, watching our little boy suffer and not being able to stop his pain.

Doctors told us in all likelihood he would not live to be old enough for a transplant. They said nothing could be done to reverse the damage. Kidneys cannot be stimulated to work after they are in failure. In the meantime, they decided he needed to begin dialysis, a very difficult and painful procedure, especially for children.

The diagnosis was overwhelming, and none of our questions were answered to our satisfaction. Refusing to accept this as the final verdict, we began to ask about alternatives and seek ways to keep our son alive and give him a decent quality of life—questions the doctors were not addressing.

Kathy began to do intense research, looking for an answer, fully intent on avoiding dialysis. She quickly discovered she was very good at it and enjoyed the effort immensely. She focused primarily on herbs and natural products, looking for something to stimulate Tristan's kidneys.

Unable to find a specific formula for his needs, but based on her intense research, she developed one. Tristan responded beautifully to these simple remedies, his kidney function improving dramatically. Though there were occasional setbacks, he grew into a tall, handsome young man. Even this was a wonderful

Change is an Opportunity

blessing as the doctors declared his growth would be stunted.

Kathy didn't stop there, however. The success people saw in her use of the formula for Tristan caused other people to ask for her help. Perhaps she could develop a formula which would help them. She went to develop an array of products which are beneficial in helping a whole host of conditions.

I realized this could become a profitable business. A business of giving people hope through natural health solutions. Starting in our garage, we developed a company specializing in herbal extracts, Mountain Meadow Herbs, Inc. We produced natural healthcare products and eventually built an amazing team to work with us.

This company, which started from zero, grew 300%-400% per year for the first four years. The fifth year it was 200%+. As you can imagine, we were very busy during that time. Today, those products serve thousands of people, improving their lives and maintaining their health. (You can read this story in Kathy's book—*A Mother's Guide to Herbal Extracts: Saving Tristan.*

iChange

The crisis of Tristan's kidney failure uncovered an opportunity we may well never have seen. That opportunity became an enterprise which has helped countless people, provided employment for a team of people, and proved to be profitable as well. The possibilities are limitless when you look for the opportunity in every situation.

> **The possibilites are limitless when you look for the opportunity in every situation.**

So many times in life, things happen which are completely beyond your control. A flawlessly executed business plan does not guarantee success for the business. Things happen. Outside factors and unexpected interruptions sometimes come into play. Such challenges also show up in your personal life, challenging your marriage or affecting your children.

When things like this happen, your natural response is fear. Experiencing or feeling fear is not necessarily a bad thing. What you do with that fear is what determines

Change is an Opportunity

your outcome. But doing what comes naturally in the face of fear may not be the best course of action. Still, it is how people often face crisis.

When circumstances cause you to have fear, it is important to recognize what is taking place inside of you before you act. Stop and ask yourself, "what am I thinking?" What are you thinking really? Your intentional thought processes will usually give you a list of options if you take the time to carefully work through them.

Many times when unexpected things happen and we are faced with changes beyond our control, we tend to feel sorry for ourselves. Things sometimes go wrong, and then the questions come, "Why did my kid get sick?" "Why did this happen to my business?" "What's wrong with me?" "What have I done?" It is entirely possible you have done nothing to cause the challenge. Sometimes, life simply throws you a curve ball.

Unpleasant circumstances are often opportunities disguised as crises. True, they are difficult and painful, costly and devastating. But they are also occasions when choices have to be made. Circumstances you never planned for and challenges you would rather not face become amazing opportunities if you let them. But those opportunities are dependent on the choices you make.

There is a big difference between simply feeling emotions and feeling sorry for yourself. You may feel sorrow or sadness when things go wrong, but don't let your emotions rule the choices you must make. Recognize the emotions you are having. Take control of them so they do not force a poor decision. This is critical in making the right choice and the having the right response going forward. Seize every opportunity for change. Treat it like a gift.

Chapter Three

Hanging by a Thread

If I thought change was going to be easy, I was mistaken. I don't really remember what I thought it would be like. I absolutely did know we would face misunderstanding and rejection. We had seen too many others leave, heard the criticisms and condemnations, and felt the contempt poured out on those who had gone before us. Still, our minds were made up.

Little did we know how severely our decision would be tested. We had no idea life would soon present us with challenges that would rock us to our very core. For the better part of a year, our lives hung between disaster and defeat. We look back today and describe it

iChange

as "our year from hell." By the time it was over, our lives were, for all intents and purposes, hanging by a thread.

Initially, breaking away from the Amish/Mennonite world was a vast relief. Having been in that culture my whole life, it is hard to describe the freedom I felt at first.

It may be hard for you to imagine, but everything I wore was scrutinized to see if it really fit the culture. This not only included what color my clothes were, but also what shade the dye happened to be. Nothing too flashy. Nothing too loud. This scrutiny is subjective. The rules are not all written, so following them is left to the interpretation of the person doing the scrutinizing.

It felt so different to be able to make decisions for our family without wondering who would be disapproving of this decision or that choice. Things went well from the start.

We moved to a new locality and embraced the obvious changes that came with the transition. We became involved in a church, one quite different from our past experience. Our new pastor was affirming and enthusiastic about my strong desire to make a significant difference in the world.

My creative ideas and desires for that future were no longer criticized and rejected. Now they were affirmed and encouraged. We were relishing in our new sense of freedom from the strictness of the past. And we were growing personally in ways we had not previously thought possible.

I landed a very lucrative contract to construct an indoor riding arena. Horses are a huge commodity in Montana, not only for work, but also for pleasure. Such arenas provided a place for almost every type of equestrian activity and constructing them was good business. I was confident such projects would propel me toward my dream rather quickly.

Our family has always been central to our dream. So having another child was a natural part of our life plan. We had named our second son Brian. After Tristan was born our doctors informed us we were not likely to have more children. It was a serious blow, but Kathy and I were unconvinced. In the Amish and Mennonite

iChange

cultures children are embraced as a huge blessing and we both love kids.

In spite of the doctor's caution, our second son was born in 1998 and now five years later another child was on the way. What joy we felt! We embraced this unexpected development as just another indication our choice had been both right and good.

Our boys joined us in our excitement, eagerly expecting another brother. Every day they talked about all the fun things they could do with their new sibling. The oldest, who usually took the lead, was excited about being able to tell another younger brother what to do!

During the third or fourth month of Kathy's pregnancy, something unexpected and terribly painful occurred. Our beautiful Labrador retriever was struck by a car and killed. He was a great pet and the boys loved spending hours playing with their dog. They were inconsolable, as children are prone to be. We all loved that dog so much and the whole family was caught up in a time of grieving.

Hanging by a Thread

Before that pain could heal completely, complications developed in Kathy's pregnancy. For two weeks we struggled, doing everything we could to preserve the life of this child. Twice, Kathy was hospitalized in attempts to prevent a miscarriage. Our hopes would rise, only to be dashed by the continuing complications. Finally the baby came, but much too early.

In spite of all our efforts, we lost our beautiful, perfectly formed little boy. For the second time in as many months, we were overwhelmed by circumstances beyond our control; this one far more devastating than the last. Kathy and I were completely distraught at the loss of our son. Our expectations had been so high and our hopes so great.

As we grieved over the loss and wept in the depths of sorrow, we began a slow agonizing descent into a dismal place neither of us ever thought we could go, or would go.

Away from Kathy and the boys, I got off by myself and cried even more. Bitter tears they were, because this was such a bitter pill to swallow. Our first son was suffering with a serious kidney problem and now this.

iChange

"God," I anguished, "How could You let this happen to us?" We had done everything we knew to prepare for this baby; had done everything we could to save him. We had been extremely careful throughout the pregnancy, but in spite of all we had done, we lost him.

Seldom can a situation be dealt with by a single choice. Seldom does a situation arise that affects only you. Others surround your life: family, friends, employees, business associates. You are never alone. Your choices usually have an effect on people other than yourself. Considering other people's needs and desires is an important part of growing as a person. Self-centered thinking always backfires in the end.

Self-centered thinking always backfires in the end.

So, what does this have to do with our crisis? Before going in for emergency surgery after delivering our tiny lifeless son, through her tears, Kathy asked me to take him home and bury him, even though she could not leave the hospital. The thought of leaving his tiny body with Pathology was unbearable to her.

So, I took him home, our Ted, for that's what we named him. I built a little wooden box, lined it with a soft baby blanket and gently laid him in it. I vividly remember sitting on the steps leading up to our house with our other boys, the tiny homemade coffin on the ground beside us. I wrapped the boys up in my arms, holding them as tightly as I could while we sobbed out our grief together.

We carried the little box around to the back side of the house and down to a creek that ran behind our home. We buried him there beside the stream. Right there with him, I buried a part of my dreams as well.

Sometimes, in spite of all you can do, you must bury a dream or lay aside a desire. But this was not my child alone. It was Kathy's and the boys' as well. It would have been easier for me to let the hospital handle this part.

Setting aside what could have been the easy route, I followed through with Kathy's request. I knew it meant

iChange

a great deal to her and I discovered it helped me cope with the loss as well. There is a balance to be struck, a balance between focusing on ourselves—our own desires, needs, and pain and helping others around us who are also in pain.

My construction business was going well enough, but it required a crew. This meant I had a payroll which had to be met every week. The income from the business was good. However, we were living in a day to day, month to month income pattern. We could ill afford to have a problem develop in the business. We had no margin for the unexpected. There was no safety net.

Then, almost on the heels of losing the baby, a client reneged on a contract. His large riding arena had been completed. But he refused to pay a large sum of money which he owed for the labor we had completed. The loss was a withering blow.

My crew had to be paid. My family had to be cared for. We were meeting the cost of two home mortgages and trying to establish the herbal extract business at the same time. The strain was more than our finances could withstand. Something had to give.

One of the houses we owned was a rental property. Actually, we had built the home and lived there for a season. Then, when we left the Mennonite community we moved to another part of Montana, and when it did not sell we simply kept that house to serve as an extra source of income.

With the unexpected financial loss, our problems mounted and things rapidly went from bad to worse. We were able to save one of the houses, but the other one we lost, along with the equity we had built there. My wife began to sink into a deep depression. Just surviving seemed to be a struggle.

Almost daily I found myself working late into the night, trying to make a success of the herbal extract business. It was a difficult time in our lives. Then, within three months of the foreclosure, just when we thought nothing else could go wrong, my father passed away. Crash!—another unforeseen, uncontrollable circumstance.

iChange

We traveled from Montana to Michigan to attend my dad's funeral. For the first time since our departure, and in the midst of deep personal crisis, we now also had to contend with facing the disapproval of the Amish and Mennonite cultures. Because we had left them, we were exiles. We were not totally ignored, we were simply surrounded by disapproval and scorn. We had left, and we were judged to be "lost sheep."

Our clothing was no longer the distinctive apparel of the plain people. It was English. Kathy no longer wore a traditional head covering which caused her to stand out in an even more pronounced way. We no longer fit in with these people, and we were made painfully aware of how true this was. We had never felt more alone.

You can never completely prepare for a parent to die. You know they will, but when the time comes it's still a shock.

As I stood by dad's coffin, my tears were not so much about the loss of a loving father. My heart broke as the reality of how so much of what my father had to offer would be buried with him that day. I wept over his inability to choose to make the changes that would have freed him to pursue his dreams, to develop his gift of communication and connecting with people, and to leave an incredible legacy. Instead, his days were spent under the constant restraint of "it's not allowed."

With my two sons standing next to me, I resolved to live life fully and embrace whatever change was needed, both for their sakes and for my own.

> I resolved to live life fully... and embrace change...

My father's gifts and skills were created as a part of him. He was never able to develop or utilize those gifts to their fullest capacity. Things I know he wanted to do, he didn't do because they simply were not allowed by his culture, his community, or his religious commitment. That, I believe, was the underlying cause of his frustration. It was a great loss to the community in which he lived and worked.

iChange

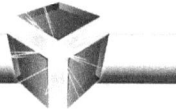

Not doing what you were created to do will always leave you frustrated and unfulfilled. As a young man, I always felt I was created for something I was not allowed to do. This was incredibly trying and unrewarding, especially when I was convinced I could do nothing about it.

Realizing I can choose to change and finding the courage to move toward that change has been liberating and very satisfying. Granted, the changes I had to make were huge. But without them, I would not be where I am today, and I might still be constantly looking at the backside of a mule.

The changes I had to go through to grow personally were not always pleasant. In the end, however, they were far less painful than not being able to do what I was created to do. To me, this would be the saddest outcome to my life. I do not want to die knowing there are things I could have done if only I had been willing to change.

Hanging by a Thread

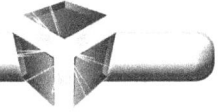

In the face of this mounting parade of problems, our minds became plagued with doubts about our decisions. We plied ourselves with questions and challenges. Perhaps they were right. Maybe we were destined for failure. We had left on our own, against every admonition by church, friends, and family. Maybe this actually was God's way of punishing us for going astray. Would it have been better to stay?

It was at that point, when we were literally hanging by a thread, that I made a choice to hold on to my decision. We would not quit! We would not give up! I had buried a part of my dream with my son. I had buried my dad, whose dreams would never be fully realized.

My dream, my real dream of making a massive difference was still alive. We would focus on what was working and find ways to fix

> **We would focus on what was working and find ways to fix the things that weren't.**

iChange

the things that weren't. After all, our dreams, our lives, and our children's futures were at stake.

Every intentional change you make to improve your life or alter your situation will be tested, some more severely than others. Some tests will be brief and relatively easy. Others may be intense and take months or even years to get through, but you can get through them. Some tests may need to be repeated several times, as you work through the process of change.

Your situation will be different from mine, but you can be assured you will face your own situation. The important thing is you don't give up. Push through, regardless of the difficulty. Your dreams and desires are at stake. If you give up, they will never be fulfilled.

You may not have to make far-reaching changes like I did to find your fulfillment. You will have to make changes, however. Success is never a given. It takes effort, and it takes a willingness to face circumstances with courage and determination.

The changes you face will not always be pleasant either. In fact, some of them will be very hard and will carry very real challenges and consequences. But in the end, making a necessary change moves you forward toward the accomplishment of your goals and the fulfillment of your dreams.

Healthy change is a vital part of personal growth. It's not about running over people to get what you want. Neither is it about what the people closest to you think.

Healthy change is about taking an honest evaluation of your life to determine if you are on the right course. It's about knowing where you want to go and what you are willing to do to get there. It's also about having the courage to make tough decisions when you face challenges, or when you are faced with a decision that violates your own sense of what is right or wrong.

iChange

It doesn't matter if they are personal changes, business changes, or changes that take you to a new place in life. You are the one who must choose which steps you will take to move forward. Refusing to change will keep you trapped in that place of not doing what doing what you were created to do.

> **Refusing to change will keep you trapped in that place of not doing what you were created to do.**

Chapter Four

Enduring Change

Change is obviously a process. The question that arises is can you process the change? Can you "hang in there" until the change takes hold? And if you do, will the change last once it has been made? Enduring change means both at the same time—hanging in during the transition and making changes that endure the test of time.

When you have made the decision to go with your dream, you generally don't know how long you will have to keep at it until success is in your hands. Sometimes, you have to enjoy your dream in "chunks," smaller pieces that come together as you wait and work toward your goals.

iChange

I have made a host of small changes during my lifetime. I've also made some large and extremely difficult ones. The lesson I've learned and continue to learn from this is to go "all in." Life is not a test. It is an interesting journey. It happens, and you cannot simply step out of it when things are not going the way you like them to. So, go all in.

> **Learn to see things through even when they become unpleasant.**

Make the commitment to yourself to develop staying power. Learn to see things through even when they become unpleasant. It is the perspective of success.

A proper perspective is vitally important when situations become difficult. You need "staying power" to weather the storms of life. You need a different perspective than *my life sucks right now.* It may, but it is not the final verdict on your future.

I know of no substitute for purposing in your heart to come through whatever you face at the moment. There will be times when you feel overwhelmed by

Enduring Change

circumstances, I am sure. Most people do. But, don't stay overwhelmed. Find a way to get motivated and mobilized again. What you sincerely don't want to do, is to do nothing.

When you feel your life is caving in, refusing to act is disastrous. You can correct a wrong decision. You cannot do anything with a non-decision. The paralysis of indecision is what keeps good decisions from surfacing in times of crisis and negative circumstances. You must remember, this is your life. This is the real you in the need of forward movement.

Get up! Call a friend who will allow you to complain and whine a bit. Call someone who will let you get it out of your system, then pull you back and say, "What do we need to do to help you get back on a positive note."

One year, we had a great deal more trouble than usual managing Tristan's kidney problem. He was in and out of the hospital, once with a strep infection, wreaking more havoc in his already damaged kidneys. At times it took days to find an antibiotic that would clear the infection. It was so hard not to fall into discouragement. We had worked so hard, and the early results had been so good. Now, it seemed things were failing. Discouragement began to rise and the temptation to give in was real. Not good for Tristan; not good for us either. Still, it was disheartening to see him suffer one infection after another.

My wife and I had friends we often called during that time. Ben and Carolea Burdick and Doug and Cindy Miller could be counted on day or night to be there when we needed them. These caring friends would offer a word of encouragement and pray with us, and for us. Because of them, we didn't feel like we were alone in our trouble. Their encouragement helped us gain the resilience we needed to keep fighting the infections and the sickness in our son.

Never underestimate the value of friends and associates.

Never underestimate the value of friends and associates. We were created to live in relationship with others like ourselves. Trying to stand

Enduring Change

alone against the stresses and frustration of defeating circumstances is an exercise in futility. Especially when you can have people around you who will help you carry your load by encouraging you and being involved in your struggle.

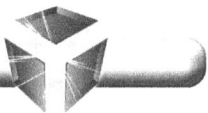

During the first years of building Mountain Meadow Herbs, Inc., I worked diligently with my construction company during the day. In the evenings, I would go into a room we had registered as a commercial kitchen. There, I would work until one or two o'clock in the morning, developing that business as well. Day after day, week after week, I would put in the long and tedious hours, so exhausted at times I thought I could not go on.

Then I would tell myself *this is only temporary, one day it will pay off.* I had no doubt the herbal extract company would grow faster and larger than the construction company. So, I endured those uncomfortably long hours because I totally believed it would bring me to what I desired and expected in the end.

iChange

I could have been resting on the couch, watching television, and sipping iced tea. Instead, I returned to the kitchen again and again, working until midnight and beyond. Some things in our lives cannot be accomplished by any means other than old-fashioned hard work.

While it may not be physical labor, it may well mean laying aside some leisure time. It may mean not doing what you feel like doing in order to obtain the outcome you desire but do not currently have. The single most destructive thing people face today is not having the discipline to put off doing the fun, easy thing in order to get the important things done.

> **The single most destructive thing people face today is not having the discipline to put off doing the fun, easy thing in order to get the important things done.**

Positive change that lasts is as important as not giving up when you are in the middle of change. It is tempting to skip key steps when you're choosing to make necessary, but unpleasant changes.

Enduring Change

You want to receive the greatest results for enduring the pain of going through. Don't try to take a shortcut through the process. Be thorough. Be exacting. Be tenacious and see things through to the end.

No one wants a surgeon to leave a portion of a tumor inside their body. Hurrying through a surgical procedure is foolish. You expect your doctor to be both thorough and complete.

Why would you not be thorough in all areas of life and completely remove those things that need to go? It only makes sense to rid yourself of the things that keep you from the life you desire.

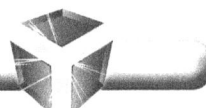

Our lives have changed in amazing ways because we have learned to rid ourselves of hindrances. We constantly monitor our lives to protect against harmful attitudes, limiting behaviors, and challenging habits. More rewarding than that is to see our son, who has grown into a young adult, make hard, beneficial choices much as we have.

iChange

As humans, we model what we see. Whether it is our parents, our associates, or our friends, who we "hang with" is important. We need to know they have the type of life we desire. Are they content? Are they happy? Are they successful, considerate, and industrious?

If you truly want change to last, you must endure the struggle change requires. The specific things you need to address in your life can be revealed in part by the attitudes and behaviors within your sphere of influence. It may be your family or an organization you lead. If their values, perspectives, and behaviors do not reflect those you hold for yourself, you may be part of their problem. This could be a great indicator of some of the specific things you will benefit from in addressing your own life.

> **If you truly want change to last, you must endure the struggle change requires.**

Chapter Five

Evaluating Yourself

When things happen that are out of your control, as they do to everyone, you have choices to make. How you go through those situations marks the difference between success and surrender. And how you go through is always a result of the choices you make in the circumstance.

It is easy to come to a conclusion you are doing things wrong when you may not be at all. At times like that, you are tempted to quit—to lay down your dream and back away to a more comfortable, less troublesome place.

In times like this, it is greatly beneficial to become something of a second party within your own skin.

iChange

Learn to stand apart from yourself and evaluate your circumstances as though you were not affected by them. It will help you be free to critique your own actions to determine if they are creating or contributing to your problem. While your answers may not change the circumstance you are in, they will help you decide your course of action for the future. By thinking through questions like these, while standing apart from your initial response, you can control your emotional reaction and give yourself a better sense of direction.

Are your actions creating or contributing to your problem?

If you will stop and reflect on these questions and others like them, you will have much better success thinking through difficult situations in the future.

→ **When negative things (which seem to be out of your control) happen to you or your business, what is your response?**

You may or may not be part of the problem. Determining if you are will help you face your problem. You must certainly be part of the solution.

Evaluating Yourself

→ **Can you identify specific thought patterns or habits you have?**

People often overlook the part they play in bringing certain circumstances to pass. When your thought patterns are negative or your habits hinder your progress, change becomes necessary to move forward.

→ **Were the thought patterns and habits beneficial or harmful to your life or business?**

The honest evaluation of those patterns offers a strategy for change. Looking at the results of your thoughts and habits allows you to determine which parts of them were harmful. The strategy then becomes a plan to conquer the weaknesses and maximize the strengths.

→ **Did those patterns open a door for your circumstance to improve?**

Though you may not have created the situation, your initial and ongoing responses have a definite effect on the outcome. A conscious effort to meet circumstances with a positive outlook and a solution minded approach will keep them from becoming worse. Now you can work to make them better.

➡ **Do you become resourceful and find a way through or around the problem, or do you concede to the circumstance and hide from the future?**

The answer to this question will determine your success or failure to move past the situation.

Unforeseen challenges and out of control circumstances are critical times. They disrupt your plans and oppose your dreams, especially when you have to make difficult adjustments to get to a specific point in your life. You think you're well on the way to achieving what you wanted. Life is going well. You can see the point of arrival in the process, the fulfillment of your goals coming closer and closer. And then—bang! The bottom drops out.

This is when you must make the hard choice. Either you can retreat within yourself and complain that life isn't fair and stuff like this always happens to you. Or,

Evaluating Yourself

you can repeatedly ask the unanswerable question, *Why does it never happen to other people?* even though it does. Or ...

... You can embrace the situation and move forward. You can say, "Wow, this is really painful. I did everything I knew to do and it still fell apart. I won't quit, though. I'm gonna hang in there because I know my day is coming. I may be down, but I'm not out. I'm a first class, fully committed, determined success story in the making. This will pass, and I will go forward."

Talk to yourself. Your inner dialogue is very important, because it establishes the foundation for what you really believe in this circumstance. Your inner dialogue is the conversation that goes on in your head, your self-questioning, your self-criticism, and your self-encouragement. But only you have the power to determine what your dialogue will be.

Everyone has internal conversations, consciously or unconsciously. Your self-talk can either fortify you or undermine you. So control it. It will actually determine how quickly you can move beyond something which has taken place.

iChange

If you struggle to control your inner dialog, change the atmosphere around you. Listen to music that moves you into a positive place. Go for a hike to change your surroundings. Discover and surround yourself with whatever it is that inspires you to keep going forward.

Realize the times of hardest trial are your greatest opportunities to build emotional strength... endurance muscles in your mind and will. The patience you learn will be invaluable. These times smooth away the hard edges on your character, giving you the ability to better embrace change.

It's a process that takes time. It usually involves pain, especially when circumstances spin out of control and you face criticism, rejection, and misunderstanding. However, if you don't remove yourself from the process, you will grow. You will grow immensely, and your life will change for the better.

Evaluating yourself also requires you to maintain a detached curiosity about yourself. Stay in the game. Ask yourself questions to which you must search to find answers. Allow this "second person" in your inner dialogue to be a curious bystander who is trying to help

Evaluating Yourself

you find your way through. Evaluate yourself from a perspective outside of your own skin.

Why do you feel and act the way you do in certain situations? What can you change to make your character stronger and your personality more agreeable? What lessons can you learn from a season of difficulty you have gone through?

Do not be afraid of self-evaluation. It is not a test you pass or fail. It is a test to strengthen your character, deepen your perspective, and develop strategies for greater success. Honest self-evaluation becomes an ally rather than an opponent.

Do not be afraid of self-evaluation.

We often find ourselves afraid of looking in the mirror of our character, emotions, and feelings. We fear that what we see will be something we cannot fix. But when you have made the decision to press through problems at all costs, fixing the problems is a must.

Then, a "life-mirror" reveals the important clues which will lead you to solutions. Finding new ways of

iChange

accomplishing your goals begins with recognizing what didn't work. Creating new pathways to success is action carved out of seeing which part of your journey was in error.

Self-evaluation is an important principle for embracing the creative power of dynamic, disruptive change. Developing the ability to step outside yourself—stand apart—and talk yourself through options and obstacles, triumphs and setbacks will allow you to fortify your resolve, build your confidence, and move forward.

In essence, you must become your own best friend—brutally honest, completely supportive, and totally committed to your own success.

Chapter Six

Engaging Your State

Do you ever find yourself wondering why the same things keep happening over and over? There are several reasons, but perhaps the biggest is your **state**. By **state** I mean **the condition your mind and will are in with regard to yourself, your world, your feelings, your thoughts and dreams, your commitments, and your inner beliefs.**

Your state determines the mental process by which you evaluate and respond to circumstances. How you process your thoughts and responses is important. What you focus on when things happen in your life—both good and bad—is crucial, because whatever you focus on, you empower.

iChange

You've heard remarks like, "he makes me so angry," or "she frustrates me to no end." In reality, short of physical torture, no one makes you do anything. Everything is a choice. But it is a natural response to blame something or someone else when things go wrong.

We seldom give much thought to our state, especially as circumstances are happening. This is particularly true when situations sour or circumstances turn negative. People project blame toward other people, making their own problems the fault of someone or something else.

People only have power over you if you give it to them.

But people only have power over you if you give it to them. By maintaining a conscious awareness of your state, you are positioned to respond positively and calmly when troubling circumstances arise. Why, because you are able to engage your state based on your chosen values and beliefs, not on a reaction to a problem.

Focusing on negative things has the ability to cause people to feel bad most of the time. For many people, depression is not as much a sickness as it is the result

Engaging Your State

of focusing on negative things or people to whom they have given power. This is so dangerous, because what you give power to has the ability to control you. If you unconsciously allow negative thoughts, emotions, and blame to govern your state, you are wide open to be controlled and manipulated by other people or circumstances.

You need to pay attention to your thoughts and feelings. Be aware of how connected they are to your circumstances. Things people say, things you see, and things you hear provoke responses in you. You can choose your response by controlling your emotional reaction, or you can unconsciously react to what you see and hear. This is what makes marketing is so effective.

Billboards along the highway, infomercials, advertising spots on TV, and the internet are designed for one purpose—to sell. They are seeking to influence your buying choices. They don't call this manipulation; they call it incentive to buy. However, those ads are designed to break down sales resistance and entice people to desire a specific product or service above and beyond others of a similar nature. That in itself is not a bad thing. It is a part of our free market system.

Advertising creates conditions whereby people can evaluate options and make conscious choices. But, impulse buying, brand identification, and peer pressure are also carefully calculated into sales equations. What people see and hear can and does influence them. People with low sales resistance usually overspend, and all too often they fall into appalling consumer debt.

If your life is or seems out of control, you are likely unaware of how much your unconscious state guides the choices you make. Your decisions govern your results. When your results consistently fall short of your expectations and plans, there's a problem. You need to step back and take another look at your process.

> **Your unconscious state guides many choices you make.**

Evaluate your state. Are you being intentional about the choices you are making? Or, are you simply reacting to things happening around you?

Engaging Your State

Consider your feelings in an honest way to determine whether or not they are being guided by circumstances beyond your control. Slow down a bit in your decision making process. Put your mind in gear, so to speak, and engage with a process that will cause you not to be reactive to a problem or set of problems.

The truth is, bad things can and do happen to good people. Across the span of your lifetime, in all likelihood you will encounter calamities, crises, and personal disasters. Everyone would like to avoid such experiences. After all, no one really wants to go through difficult or hurtful circumstances, but no one is immune. Things happen, all too often at the most inopportune times. It is during these times you are forced to make difficult, sometimes life-altering choices that are critical.

Having the emotional strength to embrace necessary change is something you need to develop long before difficult things occur. Having a solid awareness of your state allows you to engage it and respond to life as the person you have chosen to be.

iChange

I have not always made good decisions. I wish I had. In most of those situations I failed to take the time to learn all the facts regarding my circumstances. I simply moved too fast.

Sometimes, I do have the facts and an opportunity looks absolutely great, but I miss the timing. Sometimes, what appears to be a great opportunity or possibility turns out to be a flop regardless of what I do. When things like this happen I have to choose not to become a victim and fall into a negative, self-defeating state. I also have to learn from my mistakes so I will be less likely to repeat them.

After years of trial and error, I have discovered that when I make a mistake, it is not terminal. Mistakes can be redeemed, either by fixing a problem, or moving forward with the opportunities of change. So I focus on finding ways to redeem my missteps or lost opportunities. If something can't be redeemed, I move on. I don't linger for very long, wishing I had done something differently. The Pennsylvania Dutch people

Engaging Your State

have a saying—*If you "hafta" swallow a frog, lookin' at it a long time don't make it taste no better."* It simply means—don't delay, move forward!

Because of everything I've gone through, all the twists and turns and changes in my life, I very rarely give power to negative things that happen. I never think, "Oh wow, now it's over. I might as well give up and quit."

Your present circumstances are never permanent. Even when they cause permanent changes, those changes do not change the real you. So, do not accept current losses as permanent losses. The moment you do they will become permanent. Current losses can become doorways to future opportunities depending on your response.

Current losses can become doorways to future opportunites depending on your response.

Don't give credibility to the thought that because something is one way at one particular moment, it will always be that way. Things change, either on their own or because someone changes them. If your results are not what you expected, you know what to do.

Engage your state. Be empowered by what you know to be true rather than letting yourself be sapped of energy by negative thoughts and feelings. Remember—your results are always connected to your thoughts and feelings.

Are you looking at an incomplete project that is stymied? Are you trying to find the one missing piece to fix a problem, but no one is paying attention? Perhaps the problem is not the people, or the project, or the missing piece. Perhaps it is the person who is doing the looking.

Engaging your state is more than simply thinking and feeling good about yourself and your situation. It's also about being connected to the people around you. People enjoy being around people who are pleasant to be with. They don't enjoy whiners, complainers, or self-sung "know-it-alls."

This is true both in business and in social settings. People hesitate to associate with those who are ill-

Engaging Your State

tempered or ill-mannered for very long. Neither do they hang around with people who are always talking about their problems.

You should have friends who will encourage you. But if you are constantly wearing a "long-faced" look of despair, you won't have many friends. Not only that, those you do have will avoid you more than you imagine.

It is very difficult to attract quality people to your business or enterprise when you're negative, argumentative, or irritable. They might have the missing component to finish your project. They could be that necessary but missing member of your team. They will not be drawn to you if your state is undesirable to them.

Always expecting things to go wrong creates a negative state and fails to produce the results you're looking for. Focusing on the things that are going wrong without pursuing positive, innovative solutions will make it difficult for you to engage with people.

It is your responsibility to manage your thoughts and feelings, not your spouse's or anyone else's for

> **The more you learn to manage yourself, the more resourceful you will become.**

that matter. The more you learn to manage yourself, the more resourceful you will become. Learn to remain in the moment, conscious of how your state is affecting those around you.

When you're in a pleasant mood and feeling good, people will enjoy being in your presence. When you're not, don't export it. The thoughts you are having and the feelings you are projecting determine your value to your immediate world.

Recognizing when your state becomes negative is a major step toward engaging others in a more positive way. When you are aware of your immediate thoughts and feelings, you have the power to change them. If you ignore those thoughts and feelings, you will discover they have power to hurt you and others around you.

The fulfillment of your dream just might come out of the most devastating of circumstances. For Kathy and me

Engaging Your State

that became reality. Tristan's kidney problem was such a heart-rending, negative circumstance. But because of it, we grew strong as a family, determined as parents, and filled with resolve for a future with our son. This painful circumstance also provided an amazing, unexpected opportunity we totally did not foresee.

Tristan's kidney diagnosis was devastating. If our focus would only have been how terrible our lives are, I doubt we would have been able to find the answers to stimulating his kidney function and go on to build Mountain Meadow Herbs.

Achieving your dream may prove to be the result of overcoming a difficult, negative circumstance. Regardless of what difficulties you face, they will be affected by your state and whether or not you engage it.

Your dream may be to appear on stage as an actor or a singer. You may desire to have your own business, or to create great inventions. Get what and who you are going in the right direction. It certainly is not all you will have in the end, but it is what you have right now. It is that simple.

iChange

I do not have a college degree, but it doesn't mean I'm uneducated. I do have common sense and I am insatiably curious. I pay attention to what I'm feeling, and I'm conscious of what other people feel when they're around me. I know my life isn't just about me. It's about others as well. It's also about the value I can add to people's lives, and the contribution I can make in this world.

Life is bigger than you ... bigger than any one person. If by engaging your state and attending to your own thoughts and feelings you can make life better for others, you should. You must. You were created with a purpose, whether you know it or not. Who you are can and should influence everyone you meet in a positive, beneficial way. Keeping this in mind can help you maintain your state in an effective way.

> **Who you are can and should influence everyone you meet in a positive, beneficial way.**

Negative things can be perpetuated in your life if you feed them. In just the same way, positive things can

Engaging Your State

also be perpetuated and grown. These will defeat the negative things and expand your ability to reach your goals. You must fill your thoughts with energizing ideas and positive insights.

You must build good habits in your work and daily life and govern your feelings from within. If these are the things you consistently do every day, you will be amazed at how quickly things will change.

It's amazing how small choices add up to big results. When such choices are repeated day after day, the benefits soon become very noticeable. Bad choices lead to bad results. Good choices do the opposite. So place a high value on your thoughts and feelings, give them your attention and engage your state. Not only will your quality of life increase, that of the people around you will increase as well.

You will see your circle of friends grow larger and the quality of those friendships grow stronger. Your will see your income rise as you take on new opportunities and widen your circle of influence.

iChange

Your value to your business, your community, your family, and your faith will grow to a whole new level of significance. But it all is dependent on you.

Your whole life is wrapped up in your thoughts, your feelings, and your emotions. They are at the core of your being, the real expression of who you are. You are valuable. Act like it, think like it, and enjoy the journey!

Chapter Seven

Breaking the Cycle

The journey begins with a single step. The time to move forward is now! How many times have you heard that? How many first steps must a person take before something happens? Perhaps you're thinking something like, "Every time I make a move I get pushed back. Everything I do produces nothing." Right now, stop and taken a good look at why you are where you are? Be objective and honest with yourself.

So often, we're taught to be overly critical of ourselves, not directly but indirectly. Unconsciously, we find ourselves assuming the worst instead of believing something better. It's hard to give ourselves a break.

But such self-condemning thoughts glaze over reality, they don't change it.

A more effective critique is necessary, one that evaluates your choices and responses, not one that condemns your character or demeans your skills. You can move forward only if you are conscious of the mistakes you have made and are willing to adjust your behavior in those areas.

> **You must realize—you are where you are because of choices you have made.**

You must realize—you are where you are because of choices you have made. So, own your own choices. Take responsibility for your part, even in areas where it seems you have no control. The moment you say "I had no control over that," or "I had nothing to do with it," you disempower yourself.

It is possible to make unwise choices: choices that you are not proud of, or choices that have cost you time, energy, or money. It doesn't mean your character is flawed, and it doesn't mean you have no idea what

Breaking the Cycle

you're doing. What this simply means is you made an unwise choice.

You need to ask yourself, "Why did I make this choice?" Learn from it then choose differently in the future. Have a detached curiosity about all that you do. This helps you to be more objective when you make mistakes. It also keeps you from spiraling downward into negativity.

Don't take yourself too seriously. Being in a negative place doesn't help you see the answers. It only lengthens your stay in the place you don't want to be.

Moving forward can be reduced to a few simple steps. Notice, I said simple—not easy. Change is often difficult, not because it is complicated, but because it requires you to give up deeply ingrained assumptions, behaviors, and attitudes.

To move forward, your mindsets must be adjusted. You must engage your state—not just be aware of it, but in control of it. If you complicate the process, you may abandon it before you experience the benefit of change.

iChange

Below are five simple steps you can apply to any specific area you need to change.

> **Take ownership of your choices, regardless of who else is involved.**
>
> *Say to yourself, "I am where I am because of choices I made."*
>
> **Recognize reasons why you lose hope.**
>
> *A misplaced focus on what you have done wrong can derail your forward momentum. Constantly looking back at missteps, unwise decision, or poor timing will not move you forward.*
>
> **Look again at the results you wanted when you started.**
>
> *In all likelihood, the ability to have those results have not changed, only the conviction that you can reach them.*
>
> **Rekindle the fire! Allow belief and hope to rise again.**
>
> *You are only in a temporary delay. This time of difficulty is not the final answer. Your final answer only comes if you quit, or when you die. You have not done either, yet.*

Breaking the Cycle

→ **Now change!** Adjust your behavior patterns.

It's just that simple. It is easier to behave your way into a new way of thinking than it is to think or speak your way into new behaviors.

> **It is easier to behave your way into a new way of thinking than it is to think or speak your way into new behaviors.**

The changes you make must last, so continue your new behavior every day. The outcome you are seeking will grow and grow rapidly. Seemingly small things, done repeatedly over time, produce amazing results. If you consistently apply small positive changes, positive things will happen. But if you are consistently negative, negative results will be yours to endure. What you focus on, you empower.

Early in our marriage, Kathy and I built a new house. It was a cute little 1,500 square foot dwelling where we lived with our two boys. We only lived there for a year before we left the Mennonite church. Then we relocated about two hours to the north. My assumption was that we could keep the house as a continuing asset, so I decided we should rent to someone.

Not far away were some friends we knew who decided to lease our house. I was confident they were honest and would be good renters. They leased our house and we moved. Needing a home to live in, we purchased another house. Everything seemed to be going well, but after about six months, they notified me they no longer wanted the house. Unfortunately, the lease was with their corporation, not with them personally. So, when they decided to leave, they simply dissolved their corporation.

Unexpected circumstance? You bet! I was left holding two mortgages and I was not making enough money to pay both. Every month, we were going backward. We were losing money and the stress was growing rapidly. I could not find anyone who was willing to pay me sufficient rent for the property, so it sat empty. And if that wasn't enough, that unexpected financial crisis came during this time. In the end, the bank foreclosed

Breaking the Cycle

on the property, we lost the house, our equity, and all the money we had spent trying to keep it.

This was a very frustrating and painful time for me. For a while, I was angry. I had been betrayed by my friends and blamed them for breaking the lease. But as I thought it through, I began to realize something important. I had a history to be considered. This sort of thing was not new. I had made other business mistakes that cost time and money. Perhaps they were not as painful or expensive as this, but this was part of a pattern I had experienced before. Things would start well for me, but all too often they did not end well.

In this instance, I had not consulted with a lawyer before I made this transaction. I trusted these people, and I assumed they would do what was right. When they didn't, my first inclination was to blame them. However, I came to realize they were not my problem. Their lack of integrity was wrapped up in my problem, but my problem was me.

I realized something important about myself. I had a history of this sort of thing. When I got involved in projects, my due diligence was lacking. I didn't get to

iChange

know the people involved in the project sufficiently. I didn't dig into my deals very deeply. I would get excited about the outcome I expected at the expense of the potential problems I could encounter.

The adjustments I embraced have made a significant difference. First of all, I began to slow the process down. I still get excited about potential outcomes, but I also look beyond at other things. I consider the implications if things don't turn out according to my expectations. I consider my options should plans change, the business climate shift, or the people involved disengage.

These changes did not all happen automatically, or even quickly. But, by being intentional on a consistent basis, everything has changed. Things have not all gone perfectly since then. But I have been spared from a lot of grief because of the changes. My due diligence efforts are much, much better. My enthusiasm is tempered by wisdom and patience. And I no longer assume the outcome. I plan it, work toward it, and make necessary adjustments in my own efforts to make things happen.

If I had continued to be angry with my friend and continued to blame him, I would have become bitter that

Breaking the Cycle

things didn't work out. Instead, I took responsibility for my part, my lack of perspective in what happened. I realized my behavior pattern needed to be broken.

It is hard to be objective when things go wrong. You constantly want to blame someone—anyone—for what's happening. Don't do it! Take responsibility for where your life has come to, even though someone has wronged you; even though someone has intentionally hurt you. If your life is one of constant frustration, I would venture to say that generally speaking, you blame everyone else for the things that don't work out in your life.

It can be painful and difficult to look at the patterns in your life. It is challenging to notice behaviors that are not getting you where you need to be. But it is necessary to identify those behaviors so you can begin to form new

> **If your life is one of constant frustration, I would venture to say that generally speaking, you blame everyone else for the things that don't work out in your life.**

iChange

habits. Most people have difficulty accomplishing that on their own. They need help.

I found this to be true for me. In fact, it was a significant element in making the changes I needed to make. I found a mentor in Lance Wallnau. He has a unique way of gently but clearly zeroing in on what needs to change. This friend is not ordinary. He is a person who can know everything there is to know about me without judging me. He has proven himself to be trustworthy. He is also wise. He's a kind of "sounding board" I can bounce ideas off of, because he has the ability to ask me the tough questions. This is the kind of person you want to look for because you will need encouragement.

I firmly believe we were not made to walk alone. No matter how long it takes, find someone who will make the journey with you. Find a person who will encourage you without overlooking your bad habits. He or she needs to give the kind of feedback you need to empower you to break old habits.

Breaking old habits is not easy. The first step is to identify ineffective behaviors. The next is to change those behaviors. Identifying them requires you to

Breaking the Cycle

be ruthlessly honest with yourself. Changing them requires discipline, consistency, and recovery from slips and failures.

There are many tools a person can use to enhance personal growth. A wide variety of personality profiles, business development tools, and time management tools are available. These will help with both your personal and your business growth. Whatever area you need to work on, using such tools is a huge benefit. *(Look for a list of resources that have helped me in the back of this book.)*

One of the profiles I used dealt with "constraint data," the things that keep a person from success. I realized it was time to move from where I was toward where my dreams and desires were taking me. So, I chose this profile to be able to understand what hindrances stood between me and a greater degree of success.

The primary constraint on my success proved to be that I talked too much in a group. I didn't listen enough.

iChange

This did not mean I could not talk at all, or that I should only listen to other people. Rather, it indicated that I need to be consciously aware of how much I am talking. The profile indicated I need to limit how much I talk in a group, which is a choice. Even at times when I am engaged in one-on-one conversations, I need to ask questions and listen attentively to the other person.

This was a simple change, but it was very hard for me to do. I had to work at it consistently for a long time. However, because I was honestly not satisfied with where I was in life, I knew I had to change. When I look back, I can see a very tight, clear correlation between my level of income at the time I started this and two years later. In that two year period, my income grew exponentially. More had grown than just my income, though. I had grown personally.

This demonstrates the power of choices. Small adjustments made consistently over time grow into something big. If you will become intentional about your choices and be willing to remain in a state of awareness, it will change your life.

Breaking the Cycle

Choices extend beyond personal habits. You are also responsible for the company you choose to keep. Sometimes you might choose to "hang out" with friends and acquaintances who don't encourage you to do the right things. Instead they encourage you to join them in unproductive and ineffective activities. It can go as far as destructive, detrimental behaviors.

Perhaps one of the choices you will have to make is to find some new friends. It may be time to cut ties with some old friends. It doesn't mean you totally eliminate them from your life. It does suggest you may need to severely curtail the time you spend with them.

You must become strong enough to influence their lives on a positive scale rather than them to affect you negatively. It is never too late to head in a new direction. It is never so much about where you have been as it is about where you are going.

It is never too late to head in a new direction.

iChange

Focus on past mistakes only long enough to learn from them. Then, look to the future and move forward. Doing this makes progress inevitable. If you will simply implement the suggestions I've outlined in this chapter, I am confident in three years or less, you will see a radical difference in your life. You will experience a huge difference in how you feel and in the results you achieve on a daily basis.

- **Realize that you are where you are because of choices you have made. Own your choices.**
- **Look at patterns in your life and identify limiting behaviors.**
- **Don't take yourself too seriously. Being in a negative place doesn't help you see the answers.**
- **To move forward, you must engage your state and adjust your mindsets.**
- **Choose company that motivates and encourages you toward good choices and productive behavior.**
- **Remember, it is never too late to head in a new direction!**

Breaking the Cycle

- ⇒ **Focus on past mistakes only long enough to learn from them. Then look to the future and move on.**

- ⇒ **Recognize that small changes done consistently over time add up to big benefits.**

In the final analysis, you are responsible for the direction your life follows. You may not design the circumstances; you can design your response to those circumstances. Be proactive in shaping the direction of your life. Don't be passive and give in to circumstances. Don't live as though "whatever happens, will happen." This is only true if you do nothing.

The temptation to be discouraged is strong. Sometimes you feel as though nothing you do can make a difference. I've felt that way, too. Today, however, I realize just how much difference small changes make. They either help or they hinder. Little habits become deeply ingrained and eventually have a huge effect on your state. The little things you do every day accumulate into significant change over time. So rise up! Be strong! It's a new day! Your new life is just beginning!

iChange

Chapter Eight

Releasing Yourself

You is all you really have. YOU! You are the bottom line ... only YOU! Until the moment you realize change is personal, you will be at the mercy of your circumstances. Unfortunately, people do not always see change as a personal issue. Of course, sometimes they do. And when they do, they begin to make change work in their favor. This is when they are most effective at making necessary changes to their life patterns.

One of the big problems people face, however, is low self-esteem. This makes it hard to embrace change as personal. If you don't believe in yourself, who else will?

iChange

Other people usually believe in you, even when you don't believe in yourself. Still, it is a common problem to feel that you don't carry much value, or that you can't actually deliver real value to your job or your business. Your SELF is on the line at this point. That reality forces you to recognize change is personal.

Making change personal is at the leading edge of effective efforts to change circumstances, overcome obstacles, and gain victories. When you make change your personal responsibility, you disrupt the inevitability of circumstance. You make change work for you—in your favor.

> **Making change personal is the first step in making change work for you!**

What do you feel when someone criticizes work you've accomplished or writes an unfavorable report on your record? What is your response? Do you get angry? Do you complain? Do you return criticism? Do you simply give in?

Regardless of your external response, you also internalize a response. You think and feel something, and your self-talk in response can create barriers to

Releasing Yourself

future success, especially if that self-talk is negative. As you internalize negative thoughts and feelings, you begin to believe the reports you are telling yourself. If they are bad, you will unconsciously be filled with self-doubt. You'll put yourself down and diminish your inner sense of value. In other words, you can be trapped into believing the worst about yourself, instead of the best.

An unbroken line can be drawn directly from how you see yourself to where you're at in life today. If you're constantly telling yourself and other people you're a terrible person, you're probably not being very successful in life.

If you believe you're a failure, you will project it into your conversations, your relationships, and toward your business associates. "Self-destruct" will be written across your conversations, almost as though it were tattooed on your forehead. It's time to make change work for you.

All of these things are cyclical. They follow a repetitive pattern. What you focus on eventually becomes you, even when you don't know it's happening. What you talk about, think about, read about, and give your attention to is what you internalize. The more you focus on these things, the more deeply they become ingrained in your personality and presence. They become the substance of your actualized beliefs, even when your stated beliefs are different. The deeper entrenched in your actualized beliefs you are, the more you will be the fulfillment of your focus.

This is a self-perpetuating cycle, one that intensifies with time and becomes harder and harder to break out of. It works both ways. It will either be a cycle projecting you into a dynamic, successful future, or it will become a cycle of defeat. So, it is important to be very intentional in the thoughts and feelings you hang on and cultivate.

What you say about yourself to yourself is so important. Your thoughts and feelings greatly influence who you are and who you become. They also have an effect on how you deal with people whose actions and behaviors are offensive or hurtful. We all feel good when we are praised or applauded,

> **Your thoughts and feelings greatly influence who you are and who you become.**

Releasing Yourself

but when we are treated poorly, our inner self reacts, based on the self-image we have developed through our internal dialog.

For some people, forgiving those who have wronged them is not particularly difficult. For others, it is incredibly tough. Some things, however, are very hard to let go, regardless of someone's personality or their propensity to forgive. These wounds provoke inner dialog which unconsciously comes out in conversation.

Do you ever find yourself saying things you later regret? It is easy to let negative feelings slip through your personal guard and criticize, complain, or condemn others unnecessarily. Without meaning to, you can drive an emotional wedge between yourself and other people. Unconsciously you find yourself drawing further and further away from the person who wronged you, and create a relational hurdle for friends to cross. If you are engaged in business and something negative slips through, you can sabotage a contract, or wipe out a sale without really understanding why.

What thoughts do you have when something goes awry? What goes through your mind when you are held responsible for something you believe is not your fault? Do you project blame on someone or something else? Do you criticize your company, your boss, or your co-workers for some supposed shortcoming on their part? Or, do you recognize and take ownership of your part in blowing a deal, losing a sale, or alienating a friend?

When you discover your part in defeating your own best interests, it becomes crucial for you to release your "self" from that bondage. It may be difficult to see this as a constraint on your progress, but believe me it is.

Do not begin with what other people say about you. Begin with what you say about yourself. I once heard a man say, "You will not believe what you hear me say, you will only believe what you hear yourself repeat of what I have said." It is so true. You must process information you receive, whether it is spoken, read, seen, or felt. Your process will determine your response.

If you are continually affirming yourself, saying good things about yourself, you will see yourself in that light and take pride in your contribution. What you think and say of yourself needs to be true, or if not

Releasing Yourself

immediately true, you are diligently working to make them be true.

It seems more people speak negatively to and about themselves than the other way round. There is an inner resistance to self-confidence that causes people to draw back from their best self. As a general rule, people don't look at situations objectively and say, "I will find and do what it takes to have a different outcome," and then move on. They look at momentary situations as though they were permanent, as though nothing could be done to change what they see.

> **There is an inner resistance to self-confidence that causes people to draw back from their best self.**

It's also important to release yourself from the responsibility to judge other people's mistakes and correct everyone else's errors. When you've been wronged, unfairly judged, or criticized, you need to have a statute of limitations on your hurts. Learn to forgive. Learn to let things go and move on with your life.

iChange

Remember, you are the only person you can change. You cannot change other people and you should not try to do so. Help them change, yes ... if and when they express an honest desire to change. But do not try to change them.

When you make a mistake, forgive yourself. When you say something you should not have said, causing pain or misunderstanding, make it right. Seek out the person you have wronged, ask for their forgiveness. Then, forgive yourself and move on. If they refuse to forgive you, forgive yourself anyway. Don't get stuck on their negative responses.

By forgiving yourself I don't mean simply ignore what has occurred. I mean stop. Ask, *what can I learn from this?* Seize that knowledge and learn from the moment. Then, drop it completely. Focusing on your bad and wrong behaviors has never produced good results. You were created for good. You were created to do good.

You were created to fill in the missing pieces in other people's lives around you. You were born with a capacity for greatness and the ability to achieve it. Only

Releasing Yourself

what you do with that knowledge will determine how far you take it in life.

It does not matter what your vocation is, the difference you bring to the lives of people around you is absolutely profound. Every day you have opportunity to speak encouraging words to others. You have the privilege to help someone you meet through a hard time in their life. You have the ability to instill confidence and courage in those around you simply by being courageous yourself.

You were created to make a difference in this world. To do that, you must release yourself to that potential. If you have been caught in spiraling cycles of diminished self-esteem and negative self-talk, release yourself. Get rid of those feelings of despair. Take on the challenge of becoming the very best YOU you can be. Make change work for you!

You were born with a capacity for greatness and the ability to achieve it.

Chapter Nine

Created For a Purpose

Here's a very important thing to note. You were created with a purpose in mind. I know some people do not believe that, but I must. There is more to life than me—my family, my desires, and my dreams. The world is vast and people are everywhere. Your life, your desires, your successes, and your failures affect people other than you all the time. Living with a purpose in mind, with a fully engaged positive state, and a desire to succeed is important. Only then will you be able to engage with what you were created to do.

Healthy change is a vital part of personal growth. It's not about running over people to get what you want. Neither is it about what the people closest to you think.

iChange

Healthy change is about taking an honest evaluation of your life to determine if you are on the right course. It's about knowing where you want to go and what you are willing to do to get there. It's also about having the courage to make tough decisions when you face challenges, or when you are faced with a decision that violates your own sense of what is right or wrong.

Take an honest evaluation of your life.

- **Am I on the right course?**
- **Where do I want to go?**
- **What am I willing to do to get there?**
- **What tough decisions separate me from doing what I need to do?**

Life does not stop for your convenience. When changes happen that are out of your control, life continues to go on. It's very important you continue to go on as well. No matter what you have experienced, no matter what you have faced, someone has experienced something harder than you. Someone somewhere has struggled and won. You can too. So take heart and lift up your head. There is someone who will stand with you. People everywhere face hardships and get through them. You will too.

Don't miss your opportunities for growth. You must continue to grow on a personal basis. Your progress, your income, your influence, and all the other things you want only happen as you continue to grow. In large measure, growing personally is a result of what you do with change. Whether you need to make small, subtle changes, or are forced to make huge, life-altering ones doesn't matter. The real test is whether or not you are willing to make the necessary adjustments; that you are willing to handle change effectively, so you can end up where you want to go.

Don't miss your opportunities for growth.

Not doing what you were created to do will always leave you frustrated and unfulfilled. As a young man, I always felt I was created for something I was not allowed to do. This was exasperating and unrewarding, especially

> **Realizing I could choose to change, and finding the courage to move forward with change has been liberating and very fulfilling.**

when I was convinced I could do nothing about it. Realizing I could choose to change, and finding the courage to move forward with change has been liberating and very fulfilling. Granted, many of the changes I had to make were huge. But without them, I would not be where I am today. I might still be looking at the back of a horse.

The changes I had to go through were not always pleasant. Some strained relationships, others provoked criticism and condemnation. Still others were filled with emotional pain and loss. In the end, however, the pain I endured with change was slight compared to the lingering pain of not being able to do what I was created to do. To me, this would be the most heartbreaking outcome for my life. I would not want to die knowing there are things I could have done if only I had been willing to change.

Created For a Purpose

You may not have to make the kind of far-reaching changes like I did to find fulfillment. You may only need to make slight adjustments. However, you will have to make changes. Success is never a given. It takes effort, and it takes a willingness to face circumstances with courage and determination. The changes you face will not always be pleasant. In fact, some of them will be down-right hard and will carry very real challenges and consequences.

In the end, making a necessary change moves you forward. It propels you toward the accomplishment of your goals and the fulfillment of your dreams. Refusing to change keeps you trapped in a place of defeat—of not doing what you were created to do.

iChange

> "Nobody can go back and start a new beginning, but anyone can start today and make a new ending."
>
> -Maria Robinson

Epilogue

As I write this, I am forty-two years old and I have so many things to be thankful for. I have been greatly blessed. But the road to get here has been a long and difficult journey. My hope in writing this book is to see you shorten the process of reaching your dreams. I believe the lessons I have learned from my experiences can help you move more easily from where you are to where you want to be.

One of the most important ways to shorten the difficult part of your journey is to cooperate with the changes life brings, whether they are planned or unplanned. Change often requires you to let go of one thing in order to reach out and take hold of another. You will never fully realize your dreams unless you do this.

I've seen a lot of my dreams become reality. I've been blessed with a beautiful family. I have a lovely wife and four wonderful children. I've been fortunate enough to make a great deal of money. And because of I have, I've also been able to give quite a bit of money away. My wife and I have underwritten the building of several children's homes in third world countries, a joy that is impossible to describe. But it was only possible because of the changes we made—the changes I have made.

Our son, Tristan spent significant time in the hospital, especially in the beginning. In spite of the pain and struggle, he developed a very tender heart for other children. Perhaps because he was suffering, he was moved by the suffering of others. Even as he has grown older, this compassion has not diminished.

Tristan's dream has been to travel and to make a difference for children all over the world. Whether they are orphans or just underprivileged children in a third world country, his desire is to affect their lives in a positive way. His dream is to help five million orphans

Epilogue

move from poverty and loneliness to prosperous, productive, and fulfilled lives. He has made the journey from thinking only about his own needs and desires to a dream far bigger than himself,

Fortunately, because of the changes we made in our lives, we have been able to travel to Thailand twice, as well as to the Philippines and Mexico. I can think of nothing better to help him expand his horizons and reach for his destiny than to actually see his dreams being fulfilled.

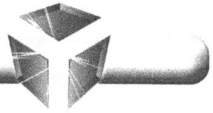

As Tristan grew, his larger size placed an increasingly strong demand on his kidneys. Finally, at age seventeen his kidney function began to fail rapidly. There was no more doubt he was at the end of his run. He would need more than an herbal formula or dialysis to sustain his life. He would need a kidney transplant.

We realized the battle we had fought since he was four was now over. The disappointment we felt was a bitter pill to swallow. But again, we asked ourselves, "What are the choices?" And we moved forward.

My wife again turned to research. She was seeking the best hospital in the nation for a kidney transplant. The one we chose was a great hospital in San Antonio, Texas. And on December 16, 2010, our son's transplant surgery was accomplished. Much to our delight, it was a smashing success.

Thankfully, as a kidney donor, I was a near perfect match. I could give him one of my kidneys, and I joyfully did so. But in some ways it was bittersweet. I had so wanted him to be completely healed, but he wasn't—not completely. At the same time, I was very, very thankful I was able to donate my kidney, rather than seeing him go through the agonizing wait, and the possibility of him not living through the waiting period.

Our second son's name is Brian. These two boys have been close throughout their lives together. The crisis in Tristan's life was also one for his brother. Clear about

Epilogue

his own purpose and direction in life, Brian began to do research on his own. He was looking for the best school—in his opinion, Johns Hopkins—to learn to be a thoracic surgeon, specializing in heart transplants.

He is passionate about justice and righting wrongs, especially in the area of health care. He dreams of generating massive amounts of wealth to fund the drilling of water wells in Africa, relieving the suffering of millions of people.

This is not his only passion, however. Right now, Brian is writing the first in a series of novels. Maybe one day you will read them, because one day, he will reach his dream.

When we lost our third child prematurely, a lot of questions flooded through our minds. The paralysis of grief and pain can stop you in your tracks, but somehow we got through it. We reached for something beyond ourselves, someone beyond us who could touch the inner core of our lives. We reached out to God, allowing our faith in His grace and power to carry us through those dark and desperate days.

While I loved and was very proud of my boys, I really wanted a girl to be my "little princess." A couple years later, Heidi was born, a beautiful bouncing girl. Another crisis, another choice—to be willing to conceive. Another miracle; we continued to grow.

Today we have a fourth child, Justin. And though he is not yet old enough to understand his dreams, Heidi is just beginning to pursue hers. At six, she auditioned to sing and dance in a professional dance group. Immediately following her audition, the leaders came to us, informing us they would like for Heidi to be part of their team. They fell in love with her stage presence and singing ability.

It is exciting for us to see her doing something she obviously loves, something which would have been unthinkable had we remained with the Amish. Had we stayed, our older boys dreams would have been in the "not allowed" category. For us, there is a deep sense of satisfaction, knowing that the difficult, sometimes

Epilogue

painful choices we made are allowing them to experience life in ways Kathy and I only imagined as children.

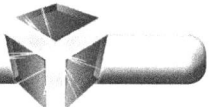

Sometimes, in choosing needed change you will be rejected by people you love and care about. They misunderstand you completely. They misunderstand who you are and where you are going. It's not easy, but the fulfillment you gain in the end, knowing you've made a difference in someone else's life, far outweighs any pain of rejection and misunderstanding. You soon realize those pains are only temporary, and though the memory lingers, the fulfillment you find replaces it with joy.

As for me, I still have big dreams, bigger now than ever. I dream of an even greater life for my family and myself. My dream will allow me to use my resources as a means of blessing other people. What began on an Amish farm years ago still propels me forward.

> **Success comes through a continuing series of intentional choices.**

Big dreams do not make you successful, however. Dreams only point the way. Success comes through a continuing series of intentional choices. When the changes those choices require you to make come together, they result in the fulfillment of the dreams you dream.

I had to learn the process of making intentional choices. Coming from a background steeped in cultural and religious tradition, choices that moved me away from that life were judged negatively and harshly. Choosing to leave the Amish lifestyle, and later the Mennonite culture was not easy. They were choices filled with challenge and dread. Our leaders and mentors filled our minds with thoughts of failure and separation from all we loved and believed. So, for me, the choices had to be intentional ones, even though at the time, I did not know where they would lead.

Today I'm more intentional about choices than ever. I have learned to step aside from the obvious while I ask

Epilogue

the important questions. I have developed a detached curiosity, searching to see if there are better solutions, better answers.

I often ask myself why I did what I just did, especially when things are not going as I expected. It's an intentional act, not something you do casually or without thinking. It requires honest self-evaluation and ownership of error.

When I do something that doesn't work I don't beat myself up over it. I don't allow myself to wonder how I could be so incredibly stupid. I acknowledge my mistake, look at the process, and ask myself why I did that. What led me to the choice to do that particular thing? Then I learn from that mistake so I don't do it again. There were plenty of times I didn't follow that pattern, but I've changed my approach. I face every challenge intentionally, so I don't repeat mistakes and waste precious time chasing ideas that don't work.

Every person who wants to move forward should become more intentional about their choices. Opportunities can come at you very fast, and the changes you face will either be the ones you choose

iChange

or the ones that choose you. How you embrace those changes is your choice. It will make all the difference in the world.

Find fresh courage within yourself and the desire to embrace change. Embrace small, simple change. Embrace dynamic, disruptive change. Learn to evaluate your life objectively and intentionally. Look at unpleasant or difficult situations and make the necessary choices to face them successfully. No matter how hard they seem, you can move in the direction of success only if you choose to do so. You can make change work for you!

Bonus Material

Resources

On the pages that follow are companies and people that have played various roles in my success. I highly recommend all of them as people of integrity that are committed to excellence and rich value in every transaction;

Lance Wallnau
Personal Transformation Specialist
www.lancelearning.com

iChange

**Verne Harnish
Mastering the Rockefeller Habits**

www.gazelles.com

Created with a Purpose

**Kathy Garber
A Mother's Guide to Herbal Extracts
*Saving Tristan***

To get your FREE copy visit

w w w . m o m s h e r b g u i d e . c o m
Use Code: NGARBER0810
or call: 888-528-8615

iChange

With a genuine passion to empower people, Nathan Garber speaks convincingly on the positive benefits of change. With stories from his Amish childhood and incredible real-life experiences, his dynamic message inspires others to break free from constraints and step into a powerful, energized life.

Nathan speaks to business groups as well as at faith-based conferences and events. If you would like to invite Nathan to speak, please contact:

nathan@cornerstoneplatinum.com
(406) 407-8604

www.ingramcontent.com/pod-product-compliance
Lightning Source LLC
LaVergne TN
LVHW052254070426
835507LV00035B/2892